How to be a
GREAT
BOSS
Without Being
BOSSY

How to be a GREAT BOSS

Without Being BOSSY

DEVLIN DONALDSON

THOMAS NELSON PUBLISHERS
Nashville • Atlanta • London • Vancouver

Published in Nashville, Tennessee, by Thomas Nelson, Inc., Publishers, and distributed in Canada by Word Communications, Ltd., Richmond, British Columbia.

Library of Congress Cataloging-in-Publication Data

Donaldson, Devlin, 1957-
    How to be a great boss without being bossy / Devlin Donaldson.
        p. cm.
    ISBN 0-7852-8259-9
    1. Supervision of employees. 2. Supervisors. 3. Communication in personnel management. I. Title.
HF5549.12.D66 1994
658.3'02—dc20   94-21555
                                                                          CIP

Printed in the United States of America.
1 2 3 4 5 6 — 99 98 97 96 95 94

To all of the managers,
who struggle as I do
to do the job effectively,
and to Carol,
without whose love and belief
I would be much less a person.
—D. D.

CONTENTS

Introduction

*B*eing a boss. Having to take responsibility for the work others perform under your guidance. If you are new to the job of being a boss, there's no time like the present to learn effective ways to do that job. If you have been a boss for years, you have everything to gain in putting forth new effort to become better at your job. There is no such thing as a perfect boss. No matter how good you may be, there is always room for improvement.

To be a great boss, you first need to be very honest with yourself about why this position of authority is so important to you. You then need to ask yourself why you should be the best at the job you can be. You can try hard to be a great boss in order to impress those you work for. Or you can do it because you care for the people who work for you and you want them to be successful in their jobs.

The real answer is probably a combination of both reasons. But if you get your priorities set up right from the beginning, you can do both. By investing in your skills as a manager and by caring about the success of those who work for you, you can easily impress your bosses. When the people who work for you are successful, you are successful.

Although being a great boss is made to look effortless by some people, it is hard work that requires planning, execution, and a willingness to take risks. In trying to be a great boss, you will have problems, you will fall short of your goals, and you will sometimes ask yourself, Why am I doing this?

But if you are diligent and faithful, continually trying to improve who you are and treating employees as people and not a means to an end, in the long run you will be able to derive great satisfaction from your work.

This book offers several ways that you can become a better manager whether you're new to the job or an old hand at it. This book in no way claims to give all the possible ways to improve, but it gives you somewhere to start.

There are three areas of responsibility that any boss must be concerned with: leadership, motivation, and development of employees. Leadership has to do with the qualities within yourself that inspire others to follow you. Motivation is your ability to inspire others to do work. Development means that you take steps to let employees know that they are valued and will be given every possible chance to reach their potential within the company.

No one will need to implement all of these ideas. In fact, no one should try to implement all of them. Examine yourself and your job functions to find the areas where you can make some significant improvement. Each and every person who manages other people will know the areas that can be improved.

Some of these ideas will probably meet with resistance—from your employees, your bosses, or even yourself. Change for anyone for any reason can be stressful. So try to make changes gradually, and talk with employees about their feelings. After you implement one idea that works, you will find a more receptive audience for your future changes. And be assured that you can be a great boss without being bossy!

LEADERSHIP

CHAPTER 1

Examine your motives

*T*o be a truly great leader, you need first to understand what leading involves.

To lead means "to show the way for or to set the course for employees by going before or along with them." You are guided by your principles. They chart the course of your life. As a leader, you are to take your employees in a specific direction. The things that you live out are the very things that those who follow you will begin to exhibit in their lives. If you are ruthless, you will begin to see ruthless behavior in employees. If you are fair, you will begin to see similar behavior in employees.

Principles

To demonstrate good leadership, you must have sound principles. What do you value? There is a simple exercise that will get you in touch with your core values. The exercise was designed by Stephen Covey, the author of *The 7 Habits of Highly Effective People*.

Sit back with a pencil and paper, and imagine that you are at your funeral. Imagine that three people are going to speak at your funeral service. One is a coworker, one a family member, and one a very close friend. Write out what you would like for them to say about you. When you are finished writing, you will have an idea about the values that you hold dear. Compare them with the way that you are currently living. Chances are, you act in a way much different from what you might wish. Bring your life back in line with the principles important to you.

Honest evaluation

Far too often we act in a way that we believe others want us to act. If you allow yourself to fall into this trap, you are being dishonest. And by living dishonestly, you will find that those who are following your lead will live dishonestly as well.

Perhaps you will discover that some things are important to you that you consider less than satisfactory. This is your opportunity to change your guiding principles. Perhaps you see your role as a boss as simply making people do what you want, or you find that you work simply because you need to have the money. If you truly feel that way and don't like it, reprioritize your life. Remind yourself of the values that you aspire to have in your life.

Integral values

These values must be present to be a truly successful boss:

- Integrity
- Honesty
- Belief in employees
- Desire for growth and success in employees

Mold these values into a primary place in your life.

CHAPTER 2

Have a long-term vision

We live in an instant society. We see something, and we want it *now!* We do something, and we want to see the results right away. As with any point of view, it has strengths and weaknesses.

Wanting to get immediate results has helped our society create a huge industrial machine. We are always looking for ways to upgrade, update, and make everything more efficient. Unfortunately, the negative side of immediate results is that people are often sacrificed along the way. If they can't get a specific task completed rapidly enough, out the door they go.

This is not to say that every person has a right to a job forever—no matter how little effort is put into the work. On the contrary, it means that if we are willing to invest in equipment to get a job done right, then we must be at least as willing to invest in the people who run the machines or do the work.

Employee support

Your job as a manager requires that you look at the people who are currently working for you, determine goals for the area you supervise, and decide if the people can get you where you need to go. Often what happens in this situation is that a manager will get goals from superiors and then begin to make immediate changes in the staff. Although there are occasions when you need to do a little housecleaning, the better course is to sit down with your group, collectively and individually, and share with them the direction you need to go. Enlist their support in meeting these goals.

Employee perceptions

From such meetings, you can gather quite a bit of significant information about how employees perceive themselves. You may have a few totally dissatisfied employees. Sometimes it is inevitable that they will leave your group. You may have people who work hard but are average, methodical workers. You may have highly talented people who lack experience or confidence in doing the kind of job that you want them to do. You may have people who need additional training before they can make substantial contributions.

Employee growth

Based on the information you gain, formulate a long-term plan to achieve your goals through the people you have to manage. Look at them individually, and determine what you can do to help each employee grow and become a more satisfied, more productive worker.

CHAPTER 3

Make your principles clear

As a boss, a person in charge of a group of people, you have the right and responsibility to set the tone for how business will be done in your area. So, dig deep down inside yourself, find out what you really believe about how business should be conducted, and then let everyone know what you expect.

Every boss has a different set of principles. One may lead the group with production as the only thing that matters. Another boss may make individual achievement the guiding principle. Yet another may make honesty and fairness the ruling values in the workplace.

Impact of others

Before you can carefully and clearly articulate your principles to your staff, you have to find out what exactly is important to you. One way to do that is to list the characteristics of your previous bosses that made an impact on you for the better. What principles have you seen in others that you want to have exhibited in your workplace?

A specific list

List principles that you want to function in your area. Your list may include honesty, fairness, the customer is always right, consistency, and 100 percent effort from employees. Are some of them similar? Try to condense the list to four or five principles.

Once you have the list, go over it with each employee individually. Then discuss the principles with the whole group. When issues come up for you to deal with, mention the principles that guide your decisions. You may even want to post them in your work area.

The heart of the job

A fatal mistake is talking about principles once and then letting them fade into obscurity. To truly communicate these principles, you must go over them again and again and talk about their applications in specific situations to keep them at the heart of your job.

As you emphasize these principles, they will soak into those who work for you. As you live them out, they will give strength to employees. And if you have adequately communicated these principles, they will go on long after you. They will become a part of the lives of those who work for you. When that has happened, you have succeeded as a leader in instilling values in others.

CHAPTER 4

Be consistent

*T*he biggest challenge that you will face as a leader is living by the principles that you are trying to communicate to your employees. The strength of your convictions and your ability to live consistently with them are directly correlated to how seriously those who work for you will take the principles.

Do as I say?

Some people actually say to their children, "Do as I say, not as I do." That attitude won't work. Observing these kids makes it obvious that they emulate behavior, not rules. Talk is cheap. Actions will always speak louder than words. If honesty at all times is one of your guiding principles, but you fudge on your reports or you don't tell the truth about a situation, all of your value-laden leadership will be for naught.

No excuses

However, with all of this talk about consistency, we need to recognize one not-so-insignificant fact. No one can always be consistent. When you have violated your conscience with a breach of principle, you must be able to admit your blunder to those who work for you. Only this kind of honesty will allow others to see you as a leader with integrity. Don't make excuses for your failure to live up to your standard. As soon as you make any violation understandable or acceptable under certain circumstances, you have opened the door to a multitude of excuses, one for everything that goes wrong. Admit that you were wrong, reinforce the fact that you still adhere to your principles, apologize for your poor example, and move on.

A sacred trust

The foundation of any good relationship is trust. Trust can be developed only by getting to know another person and being open with the other person. Once you have violated this trust or given any reason to doubt that you are trustworthy, trust has been injured. And while trust can always be rebuilt, it can never be the same as it was before the injury. If you show those who work for you that you are above having to live with the same principles that you require of them, you are violating their trust.

Trust is sacred. Treat it as such. Nurture it, develop it, and protect it.

CHAPTER 5

Be honest

O ne basic principle for every workplace is honesty. Without honesty, no real communication can occur. No respect can be built. Worst of all, no one ever knows what to believe.

Honesty is very important in praise, and it is even more important in evaluations. Sometimes the truth hurts a little, but truth will always give you integrity, it will give your words power, and it will provide a basis for trust in every relationship, including those in the office.

Praise

When praising the work someone has done, avoid using general statements: "You always do great work," or "That's the best thing you have ever done." General praise offered too often will lessen the effect of the praise, and the recipient may wonder if you really know or understand what has been done well.

Be truthful and specific in your praise. Identify tasks that have been done well, and tell the person exactly what they are. Praise people directly: "You are very good at closing a sale; that's a real art," or "You have done an excellent job at taking this project and laying out plans to accomplish the desired end."

Evaluations

Honesty is even more vital in offering evaluations or constructive criticism. If you never tell an individual about the things that are reducing effectiveness on the job, you allow the behaviors to grow and become reinforced. Often a supervisor is uncomfortable discussing areas of weakness or confronting areas of less-than-acceptable results. That uneasy feeling is not necessarily bad. It can be an indicator that the boss needs to pay special attention to the subject and deal with it honestly and positively.

Once again, avoid general or categorical statements: "You *never* do this right," or "Your work is really not very good." General or categorical criticism can be construed as a personal attack or an indication that the employee can never fix the problem.

Much more can be accomplished by saying, "You seem to have a problem in following through on a project. What do you think the problem is?" Or "I am having a problem with your attitude toward your coworkers." Don't allow feelings of discomfort to restrain your ability to tell people what you think. (Of course, a harsh approach is rarely acceptable.)

With your honest and direct communication, employees will know clearly where they fall short and where they excel. They will also know that you care enough about their work to recognize what they are doing well and not doing well. They will respect the fact that you care enough about them and their success that you pay attention, get involved, and tell the truth.

One reason you feel hesitant about delivering honest evaluation is that it is uncomfortable and sometimes people are hurt or don't respond well. But telling the truth will pay huge dividends in the long run. Be honest with those who work for you.

CHAPTER 6

Honor before honors

A boys' school in England has the following inscription above the doors: HONOR BEFORE HONORS.

This phrase is packed with meaning for life in general and life in the workplace. But to truly understand it, we need to understand what honor is. Honor is "a sense of right and wrong that causes us to act with respect and rightness toward others."

Reputation

Honor can be a guiding principle for you as a manager of people. If you treat those who work for you with respect first, honors will come your way. Why? To know what you believe in your heart to be right or wrong—and to adhere to the principles in every case—is to build a reputation as an honorable person.

Being honorable isn't always easy, and it doesn't always get you awards or recognition. But in consistently being an honorable person, you will be rewarded with the peace of mind of doing right and knowing that you have treated others as they deserved to be treated. Peace of mind is a far more valuable commodity than a plaque, a trophy, or a commendation.

Better than a trophy

There is an old saying that says: "What goes around comes around." You have to believe that by doing right, you will be treated right. And even if you are not treated properly, you will not be swayed from pursuing personal honor instead of personal honors.

Acting with honor for the long term will pay you back abundantly in the long term. Most important, acting with honor develops you as a person. You will be trusted and looked to for an unwavering view of the right thing.

CHAPTER 7

Decide

*L*ike it or not, as a leader, you are called on to make decisions—many of them each day. You will make good decisions and bad decisions. Some will solve problems, and others will cause even more problems. But you must decide.

Don't be hasty

A piece of conventional wisdom asserts, "To make no decision is to decide." When confronted with a difficult decision, you should not be hasty. But you do need to keep moving toward a decision. You must consider many aspects of a situation: How will it affect my company? How will it affect morale? How will it affect individuals involved in the decision?

Do it!

One company's managers decided to do some reorganization. They talked about it and let everyone know that it was going to happen. Then they spent the next eighteen months trying to figure out what to do. The situation created a significantly heightened sense of anxiety for employees, whether they were going to be affected or not, because no one knew what the future held. When it finally happened, the reorganization was anticlimactic. It affected a few people significantly and had little impact on most, save the anxiety they lived with for such a long period of time.

Perhaps you have a structural problem within the area you manage. You know you must reorganize several jobs to facilitate a better flow of work or a better quality of work. You know that in the reorganization, there will be some people who will feel slighted because they didn't get a promotion or their boss will be changed. Consider all the things that might happen. Get counsel from executives in your company or others who have had the same experience. Evaluate all the information you have, be prepared to make your best decision, and then *do it*.

After you have made the decision, be prepared to deal with all of the problems that you have anticipated—disgruntled workers, lower morale, a temporary slowdown—as things settle back into a working groove.

Don't delay too long

If you know what you must do but delay the decision because of the issues you will have to confront after making it, you are really saying that things are OK the way they are. The problems may grow in the time that passes, or they may not. But those who will be affected will experience a growing sense of unease and a reduced level of motivation to perform at their maximum capabilities. You will suffer from the time you know what you must do until you do it.

Admit it

So, you consider the options, think about the ramifications, and make your decision about what must be done. It turns out to be a bad decision. Own up. Admit that it was a bad decision. Reevaluate the decision, consider solutions to the problems that confront you, get more advice, anticipate future problems, and make a decision to correct the situation.

Some managers wait so long to make a decision that problems become more significant, changes are more traumatic, and work suffers in the meantime. Some managers wait so long to make the first decision that they could have decided, evaluated, realized they made a mistake, and fixed the mistake in the same amount of time.

Second-guessing not allowed

Don't be hasty, don't ignore real facts, wait until you know deep inside that you must decide, and then do it. Don't second-guess yourself or you will become an ineffective manager unable to keep up with changes in the marketplace and in the workplace. So decide, for the sake of your employees and for your sake. You can't steer a ship that isn't moving.

CHAPTER 8

The open-door policy

*T*he demands on the time of a manager are enormous. You have to spend time on budgets, personnel issues, meetings with your staff, meetings with other executives, and planning, and the list goes on. With all the various items pulling for your time, it is obvious that you must protect it and manage it.

Your time is also the one thing you have that no one else can give to the people who work for you. There are questions to be answered, crises to be handled, and problems to be addressed. How do you find the time to give all of these concerns? Sometimes you just can't. You will have to decide what things are higher on the priority list and/or work extra time to complete the tasks before you.

Prioritizing

You can most wisely invest your time with your employees. The more time you invest, the bigger the dividends. That is especially true when you are just beginning to supervise a specific area or when you have new employees who need to have your insight and your values communicated to them.

Being approachable

You need to have an open-door policy so that you are approachable. When you are approachable, you will have time to communicate your values, to train, and to teach.

Planning ahead

To have this open-door policy, you must plan for interruptions. As you make out your daily or weekly schedule, build in enough flexibility so that you can deal with interruptions gracefully, without cutting into the time set aside for matters that definitely need your attention.

How do you plan for the unplanned interruption? When you schedule your time, don't book yourself minute to minute with meetings and activities. Set aside an hour or so every day (the amount is really based upon your feeling of how much of your time is taken by interruptions), then go ahead and fill in your daily activities. If you get an interruption that throws your day off or keeps you from an activity that you have scheduled, you will know that you have some flextime available later in the day to make up for the interruption.

Stopping abuse

Some employees may take advantage of this policy. The first thing to do is to make your interruptions short and to the point. An impromptu meeting doesn't have to last fifteen minutes, thirty minutes, or an hour. You might be able to deal with the issue in a few minutes. You already have other times for personal chitchat, so get to the issue. The second thing to do is to exert leadership and point out that the employees themselves need to be making decisions. That is, in fact, why you have them in their positions. As they interrupt you for advice or counsel, point out to them the issues that you would rather they handle on their own. Make it uncomfortable for them to abuse the privilege of access to you.

There are pitfalls to having an open-door policy, but the result of not having this policy is communicating to your employees that other things you have to do are more important than they are or their issues are.

CHAPTER 9

Champion your employees

*A*ll too often in companies, there is a clear division between management and labor, bosses and workers. In many cases it is an unhealthy, adversarial relationship that needs to be changed. Employees with this attitude often have a deeply held belief, whether realized or not, that management is out to get them.

Be supportive

One way that you as a boss can begin to show leadership is to champion your employees. That means voicing your support of them whenever you can. Let everyone in your company know how valuable they are, what great contributions they make, and how deeply you believe in their talents and abilities and in them as people.

One company felt the need to provide more service to customers. The managers created a new area and put a person in charge of finding ways to improve customer service throughout the company. The president of the company talked about the importance of the new position and its function. His regular endorsement implicitly made clear the expectation of everyone in the company to show respect and give weight to the job this person had been given to do. The president championed the concept and the person, thus making the job much easier to accomplish.

Make opportunities

It can be a challenge to find ways to champion those who work for you. You have to look for opportunities, and sometimes you have to make opportunities. You have to speak out when it would be easier to say nothing.

When you are asked in a meeting to report on what is going on in your area, highlight the accomplishments of your employees, individually and specifically. The general statement "All of my people are doing great things" gives little real information. You want your people to be recognized for their individual accomplishments whenever possible.

When there are job openings suitable for your employees, go to bat for them. Encourage them to apply if they haven't already. Talk them up to the people who will be making the decisions. Not only will these employees have the chance to move up given time, but they will constantly have you pushing them to accept more challenges because you believe in their abilities to grow and continue to contribute greatly to the success of the company.

Show confidence

When you begin to champion your employees, they will sense your confidence in them. Confidence is infectious, and as you show employees that you have confidence in them, their confidence will grow. The more confident they are about their place, their skills, and their contributions, the more productive and self-motivated they will become.

Count the cost

When you champion your employees, you will lose some to other areas of the company in different or more responsible positions. This is where championing will cost you. You will be training more new people to take the places of the ones who have moved on. Sure, it is extra work, but the success of those who work for you can only make you more successful.

Be realistic

You cannot halfheartedly champion your employees. Championing people you don't believe in or ones who aren't qualified for higher level positions can only backfire on you. Your peers in the company will begin to doubt your judgment. Truly talented, hardworking people will get discouraged because you have treated them like less-deserving employees. You must be honest and realistic when championing your employees.

CHAPTER 10

Push authority down

Probably everyone has worked for a boss who had to control everything. The employees, no matter what level, were just people to go out and gather information and stir things up on the boss's behalf. Any real decision about what could or should be done rested entirely with one person, the boss. This approach does nothing to develop the employees, it can create huge bottlenecks in the workplace, delaying work, holding up progress, and it ends up overworking the boss.

Avoid supercontrol

A leader of a building company felt that everyone who worked for him was incapable of making right decisions. Workers hated for people to ask them questions. They tried to never make a decision. Work slowed down, and the company lost money because workers and subcontractors couldn't do what they felt was right—they had to wait to be told it was OK for them to do what they knew was right from the start. The result was a lot of unhappy workers who couldn't do as good a job as they would have liked to do.

Grow in trust

A good leader will grow in trust of employees and give them the authority to make certain decisions. The longer employees have worked for you and the more they have followed the principles that you have set out, the more authority you should be able to give them in making things happen without you.

Giving power to employees doesn't mean that you throw authority out to people who aren't competent to handle it or that you are uninvolved. Your involvement takes a different shape. Your job is to help employees understand their jobs and the values that you hold as guiding principles, and to check with them about the decisions they are making. Give them feedback about the decisions they made—good ones and bad ones—and work to help them see their jobs as you see them.

Some employees won't feel comfortable making decisions. Your job is to help them see that they need to take more responsibility in getting their jobs done.

Ensure training

As you begin to push authority down to the people who have the responsibility to get the job done, you must make sure that they have had the training they need to make the right decisions. It would not be right to urge new employees to make decisions before they are fully trained in the job and they have had enough time to know how the job should be done.

Some employees will never be able to rise above their insecurities. You will need to build their confidence.

Choose the right ones

Then it is important to find the right people to be in the

decision-making positions. Employees will have expectations of what they want from their jobs and what they are capable of doing. Try to raise their expectations, but understand that not all employees are equally gifted.

Accept mistakes

As you move toward giving authority to those who are closest to the customers, closest to the work, you will find that you may feel a little insecure about giving that authority away. That feeling is good. Recognize that your employees will make mistakes, especially in the beginning. Mistakes are OK. As time goes on and their experience deepens, mistakes will become less frequent, and you will have more capable and more productive employees.

CHAPTER 11

Make as few decisions as possible

W hen you push authority down, you are forcing the people who work for you to make more decisions. When you begin this process, one major temptation will be to step in and make the important decisions. This is an area where you will have to be very careful. For high-level decisions, things that you alone are responsible for, making decisions will be appropriate. But the more decisions you make, the less authority you are giving employees.

Relinquish certain responsibilities

Your main job is to manage, plan for, and support your employees. If you continue to hold the power in your office, employees will never learn to accept the responsibility of doing the complete job. They will not be ready to accept a higher level job because they haven't been trained to take on that kind of responsibility. And you will be constantly called upon to make decisions that will intrude on the time you should be spending to plan, deal with problems, and motivate your staff.

However, don't make the mistake of telling your employees that they are going to make *all* the decisions. You should always reserve the right to make certain decisions. And you cannot expect employees who haven't been asked to take on this kind of responsibility in the past to instantly rise to the occasion. You will need to have a plan that will enable employees to begin making some decisions and prepare them to make more and more decisions.

If you are doing your job in communicating your values and goals, your employees should be able to begin to implement the values in practical decisions. You should not ask them to make decisions without the proper foundation or experience.

Follow a plan

The first step in your plan should be to make sure that you are clearly communicating the principles that are important for you in the workplace. You must also be communicating clearly the final goal of the job. An employee who doesn't know the principles or the ultimate goal will be left guessing about how to make decisions.

The second step should be to discuss decisions that you normally make with employees who are in a position to make these decisions. Don't throw people without training into deep water and expect them to swim. Begin with discussions so they can understand how you think.

The third step should be to allow them to make some decisions. After the fact, talk with them about how and why they made their decisions. It will be a valuable learning process for them and for you. You will get a different perspective on decisions, and you may find that you were in a rut about how to do things.

The more decisions that you can push down to others, the more time you will have to perform and develop as a manager, not a doer.

CHAPTER 12

Demand integrity

A business relationship, whether internally within a company or externally with vendors and clients, is just like any other good relationship. It needs to be worked at, developed, and maintained. And as in all relationships, there is one key ingredient: trust.

One value that you must demand of employees is integrity. For if there is no integrity, there can never be trust.

More than truth

Integrity simply means having principles of right and wrong that define what your actions will be. If you have developed your principles that guide the direction of the workplace, integrity should be at the top of that list.

Telling the truth is certainly a part of integrity. But having integrity goes far enough to include living by commitments that have been made (even verbally), owning up to mistakes, not stealing in the workplace, and not padding bills.

Multiple relationships

Your relationship with each employee is only one of many

relationships. Each member of your team has relationships with coworkers, vendors, clients, and possibly even a large number of potential customers who have not yet committed to your product or service. Each of these groups must be able to trust the integrity of each of your employees. If they don't, they have no basis on which to continue the relationship.

Without trust, how can you be sure that employees are doing the best they can at their jobs? How can you count on them to carry out the duties their jobs demand? The answer is, you cannot.

Lapses

No one is perfect, and there may be some lapses of integrity based on lack of knowledge of a situation or an impulsive emotion. Everyone has failings. But they cannot be tolerated or allowed to continue when discovered.

If there are lapses in an employee's integrity, or if the violation is severe enough, it is time to do the employee and yourself a favor and terminate the employment. Termination does several things.

First, it makes clear to the employee that there is a problem that must be dealt with. Second, it allows you to be sure that breaches of integrity do not spill over and infect other employees. Finally, it lets your other employees know that integrity is a high value that you will not allow to erode.

Every company has policies on termination of employment. Be sure that you follow the procedures to legally abide by all laws and regulations.

CHAPTER 13

Do right

*E*very day, in personal life as well as business life, you are faced with opportunities to take the easy way out of situations. You know what you want to do, but you know that a likely result will be great frustration, extra paperwork, or criticism from others. You accepted your position, and with the benefits you gain from your position as a manager comes the responsibility to execute your duties as best you can.

Some secretaries were talking about a manager who was faced with a difficult personnel situation. One secretary finally remarked, "Well, we can be sure he will do what he thinks will make him look good, not what he should do."

No matter the cost

When faced with a difficult situation, you need to evaluate what is going to happen with each of the options you might choose. You need to evaluate the decision in light of the values that you have put into place. Then you need to make the decision that is the right one—no matter the cost.

For instance, maybe you have made a verbal commitment to a customer. Or maybe someone who is working for you has made a commitment. Then you find out that the price was figured incorrectly, but the incorrect price has already been communicated to the customer. Was the price a rough estimate or a formal bid? Rough estimates are still open to negotiation, but a bid is really an agreement.

Your job is to make the company profitable. You also need to maintain integrity and honor with your customer. What do you do?

The easy way

The easy thing to do would be to reprimand the person who made the wrong calculations, have the numbers run correctly, and call the customer about the mistake. You say that you cannot or will not honor the incorrect price. You lose a sale, and the customer may be very upset. But you will get out of hot water.

The hard way

The hard thing to do would be to talk to the person who made the mistake and determine if it was an honest mistake or one caused by carelessness and negligence. You discuss the situation, point out the error, and take some sort of action (reprimand, termination) based on what you learn. Obviously, if it is a situation where you could lose huge amounts of money, perhaps you need to review your procedures to be sure the numbers are checked by more people. Then you can call the customer, explain the situation, and state that a mistake was made. But regardless of the mistake, you will honor your commitment.

The right thing

You will probably take some heat from your bosses for

losing some money. But that employee will probably never make that mistake again. And the customer will probably offer to take another price since you were honest enough to take the loss. But your principle of integrity will be preserved, your esteem in the eyes of the customer will grow, and the employee will find ways to check and recheck accuracy.

Most important, you have lived out the principle of doing the right thing, no matter the cost, to your employees. These lessons are high-impact ones that aren't likely to be forgotten by anyone involved.

CHAPTER 14

Listen before you speak

As a boss, you will daily need to act, express an opinion, or get involved in settling a situation. Perhaps you will have a conflict between two employees. Maybe it will be a conflict between your department and another department in the company. Maybe you will be asked your opinion of a new product or service. Maybe you will have an employee with a personal problem. Or perhaps an employee will share a new idea with you.

Gather information

Regardless of the situation, there is one very important rule to remember: listen before you speak. Don't make a hasty decision, and don't offer advice before you have all of the facts. Get to the bottom of a situation before you make a judgment about what you or others are supposed to do.

If there is a problem between two employees, find out each side of the story. If you don't think that you are getting all of the facts, ask questions and then *listen* to the answers. Talk with both people, and then talk with others who may have insight into the situation. Information is the most important commodity that you can accumulate, and to act before you have all the information is to seriously jeopardize your ability to make a correct decision.

Concentrate on the speaker

Listening is a very powerful tool. One manager who was faced with a complex situation called in the employee involved, asked a couple of questions, and sat back to really listen. After the employee talked awhile about the situation, the employee identified the problem and offered a solution. The manager didn't really do anything to effect change but listen. This result is not the rule, but it illustrates the power of concentrated listening.

Practice

Don't make the mistake of believing that listening is easy. It is not. It takes strength of character, discipline, and time. Becoming a good listener will take practice, practice, and more practice.

There are some exercises that you can do to work on your listening skills. The more you practice, the better you will become. One thing you can do by yourself is to consciously tell yourself at the beginning of a situation that you will not say anything. Concentrate on not opening your mouth except to ask questions and clarify what you are hearing.

Another thing you can do in a small group is to pick a subject. Let someone talk about his feelings on the subject. Then pick a person in the group to repeat back to the speaker what she thought she heard him say. As you practice this exercise, you will find that listening is not being still and quiet. It is an energy-consuming activity. If you begin to get fatigued, you know that you are really listening.

We hear constantly that we are living in an information society. Although that is true, it doesn't apply just to computers. Because we have come to lean on these automated information processors, we have begun to lose our ability to gather information on our own. So, when you're confronted with a problem or new idea, get to work and listen up.

CHAPTER 15

Infect your employees with enthusiasm

*T*o have employees who are highly enthusiastic about their work, you need to be enthusiastic about *your* work. If you are like most people, that is not something that will flow out of you naturally. You must make a conscious decision to be enthusiastic. If you are a person who is naturally enthusiastic all the time, relax and be grateful for the gift. If you aren't, get ready to do some more work.

Determination

Each day when you enter the office, you must determine that you are going to be excited about what you have to do. That doesn't mean you are going to love everything you have to do that day, but that does mean you will attack each and every task with enthusiasm, whether you feel it or not. And you are going to go out of your way to find things in the workplace that are running smoothly and encourage employees who are responsible for them. You are going to spread the news of good events throughout your team so that they can be excited about what others are doing.

When you have employees who are struggling, you are going to encourage them, motivate them, and get them excited about the contribution they can make to the ultimate goal of the jobs to do. Some organizations spend great amounts of time and money trying to develop this very quality.

Energy

Take a look at sales organizations. They have regular sales meetings. Multilevel marketing organizations have regular meetings to talk about how well things are going. They herald the accomplishments of others, celebrate, and charge each other with great enthusiasm for the job that they have chosen to do.

Enthusiasm is contagious. It is not, however, a giddy, childish attitude. It is directed and focused energy. When you are unable to generate enthusiasm, it is probably time to take a break or a vacation, or maybe it is time to look for a new position, either within or outside your present organization. If you cannot be enthusiastic, those who work for you will not be enthusiastic, and that can create a downward spiral.

Conduct meetings to talk about goals and accomplishments, encourage those who are down, and generally try to focus positive energy on every situation.

CHAPTER 16

Encourage your employees to make mistakes

*E*ncourage your employees to make mistakes? That must be a misprint, right? Mistakes don't do anything but get everyone in trouble. How can making mistakes be a good thing for employees, bosses, or companies?

These questions are natural, but the answer is simple. If employees are empowered to do their jobs and they are exercising their power, they are going to make mistakes. If they sit back where they are comfortable all the time, they will never make mistakes because they aren't taking any reasonable and informed chances.

The competitive edge

We live in a highly competitive world where everything seems to be in a constant state of flux. If our companies are going to remain competitive, we are going to have to change with the times. As a manager, you are not going to have the time to keep up with all of the changes in each area that you are charged to supervise.

So you want to have employees taking initiative, trying new things, and experimenting. And when they do that, they are going to have weak ideas from time to time.

Let's look at a sports illustration. A baseball player is considered highly effective and is highly sought after if he gets a hit one out of every three times he goes to bat. A basketball player is a great shooter if he hits over 50 percent of his shots. A quarterback is very effective if he completes over 50 percent of passes.

If we look at these athletic performances, we can see why it is so vital to allow employees to make mistakes. First, it encourages innovation. Second, the production of the passes that a quarterback does complete more than makes up for the ones that hit the ground without finding their intended target.

A productive approach

The more chances someone takes, the more likely it is that some of them will work and be highly productive. Good ideas can be so productive that I would even go so far as to say you should reward people for making good attempts, even if those attempts should end in failure. You'll know that they are thinking about what they are doing and trying to do it better.

You shouldn't tolerate the same mistake made repeatedly, though. That shows a lack of judgment, an inability to learn, or just plain carelessness. You should discuss every mistake with employees and be sure that they understand what went wrong and that they have learned something from each attempt at a new idea.

Failure is a scary thing. If you encourage experimentation, you have to face your fears, but you will reap the benefits by leading your employees to new levels of effectiveness.

CHAPTER 17

Set high standards

*T*here is one sentence that cannot be tolerated in the workplace. It is very damaging to the continued growth of the employees, the managers and, ultimately, the company. That sentence is, "That's good enough."

A manager threw out a brochure design and asked the designer to start over following a brief conversation. The manager asked some questions about the design, and the designer told the manager, "Well, it could be fixed, but I think it will work good enough the way it is." The comment illustrated for the manager an attitude that he would not tolerate.

No complacency

You should never allow employees to think that what they have done is good enough. If something is good enough, it needs no improvement, and its current state is accepted as perfect. Complacency will set in. Every endeavor can be more efficient or less expensive.

Setting high standards does not mean that you berate the accomplishments of your employees. In fact, the opposite is true. You celebrate the successes and improvements that individuals and teams make in a product or service. You reward their progress. But then you move the mark a little higher so that they have something new to shoot for. A new goal is a motivator, and as a leader, you have the job of setting and resetting goals as needed.

An NBA idea

Pat Riley, former coach of the Los Angeles Lakers, during the 1980s had arguably one of the best basketball teams ever assembled. After they won a world championship, Riley knew that they wouldn't be as hungry for success the next year. The loss of drive was a main reason that no team had repeated as an NBA champion since the early 1970s.

So to motivate his players, he quantified as many aspects of each player's game as he could. Points per game, number of assists, free throw percentage, turnovers per game, and blocked shots—all were categories that he measured. Each player knew what level he played the year before. He was given the challenge to better himself in each of these areas. They didn't win the championship the next year, but many of the guys on the team knew that they had played better than ever before and had contributed to the success the team did have.

Improvements

High standards weed out complacency. They force people to constantly improve on what they have done before. Celebrate accomplishments, encourage your employees, but always set the standard a little higher.

When people feel appreciated and find that they are doing things better than they would have ever believed they could, they will usually rise to the challenge of doing a little bit better.

When things are being done "good enough," everyone will

become complacent, and the constantly changing world will quickly catch up to you and pass you by. Customers are obviously attracted to the best product or service they can get, and usually, they are willing to pay a little more for something of higher quality. So setting high standards doesn't help just you or your employees; it helps the company become more profitable as well as gain a reputation for being at the top of the game.

CHAPTER 18

Persevere

W e have talked about giving employees the chance to fail. But you need a similar attitude toward yourself. It is easy to go to a workshop or conference or read a book like this and get enthused about all the things that you can do to be a great boss. When you return to your workplace and try to implement some of these changes, remember this: you are going to fail. Not all the time, and not in the long run, but you are going to make mistakes and have difficulties in making some of these ideas consistent parts of your work life.

That's OK. Falling short of a higher standard means you are trying. It also means that even though you may fall short, you will do better than you would have done had you not tried. Every mistake is an opportunity—an opportunity to learn, to grow, and to become better.

No status quo

So when you have your first failure, celebrate it. Reward yourself for not accepting the status quo and pushing yourself to do something unique and innovative. Then evaluate what happened and learn what you did wrong.

Even if you are trying to be a more consistent manager, realize you will never be totally consistent. But the recognition that you have been inconsistent is a step in the right direction. Many people go through life and never realize that they have been falling short. They stay stuck in the same rut and can't see that they could be doing better.

The real payoff

To continue to make strides to be a great boss, you must have enough perseverance to keep going in the face of your mistakes. That takes willpower, discipline, and determination. And if you think that you don't have these qualities, you can develop them. Just keep going. Evaluate what is happening, make corrections, and have enough respect for those who work for you to be honest with them about your shortcomings.

If you can learn anything from this book, it is that being a great boss is work. It is not a quality that some people are born with and others can never obtain. A strong work ethic can help you learn all the necessary skills to be a great boss. Some have a more natural affinity to these skills and won't have to work as hard to refine them. Others may have to work harder, but the success will be all the sweeter when it's attained.

MOTIVATION

CHAPTER 19

Be a cheerleader

Nearly every team sport in America uses cheerleaders. Many people have come to believe that cheerleaders have little to do with the game. But they are an integral part of what everyone calls the home team advantage or home field advantage. What gives the home team an advantage? Things like knowledge of the field and comfort in the environment are very helpful to the home team. Another great advantage is the large group of supportive fans cheering the team on.

The job of the cheerleaders is to get the enthusiasm of the crowd focused on the team and the players' accomplishments. Also, when things are going badly for the team, they know that if everyone else is against them, the cheerleaders will still be rooting them on to victory. That is also the job of the manager in a business situation.

The groups

A great boss is a cheerleader to two separate groups. First of all, the boss is supportive of the home team, the employees. They know that no matter how difficult things get, the boss will always be cheering them on to victory. The boss isn't going to be swayed like fickle fans to change sides when the going gets tough. Such encouragement is invaluable to team members. The motivation is to work harder and overcome the obstacles that stand between them and victory. They want to justify the loyalty of the cheerleader.

The other group of people includes executives the boss reports to. They need to know that the boss is behind the employees regardless, ready to cheer for them even when they have made mistakes in the course of the game. The boss will focus the support and attention of the executives on the team that is attempting to win a highly competitive game.

The moves

But how does a cheerleader go about performing this all-important task? It is probably more instructive to look at how cheerleaders *don't* do it. Cheerleaders are as aware of mistakes as anyone in the game. They don't ignore them. They don't single out a player who has made a mistake and lead jeers deriding the incompetence of the player.

They are involved, watching and encouraging the team to success. They don't hide in the locker room. They cheer for everyone to do their personal best. When a player makes an outstanding play, they cheer wildly. They all work to instill confidence in the players on the field.

The very same principles are involved in being a cheerleader in the workplace. A great boss cheers for the home team, the employees. Individuals aren't singled out publicly for making mistakes. When someone is involved in a good deal or makes a great decision, a great boss lets everyone know about it. A great boss doesn't give up on employees because of a mistake. A great boss encourages them to overcome the bad feelings and perform up to their potential.

By trumpeting the successes of employees to higher rank-ing executives, a great boss builds in the leadership confidence that a talented and winning team is on the field and will get the job done, even if members have suffered a temporary setback. To do this effectively, the cheerleader must be watching the game. A great boss must admit when mistakes have been made but find the correct encouragement to offer.

The little victories

By finding the little successes, a boss can be a cheerleader who will build confidence and loyalty in employees. A touchdown would be great, but a ten-yard run is certainly worth cheering about. If employees become confident that their little victories will be recognized, they will put lots of little victories together for a big win.

So take it as a part of your job as a boss to create a home team advantage for your employees and cheer them on.

CHAPTER 20

Make recognition a regular event

*I*n recent surveys, pollsters have been trying to find out exactly what motivates employees. In our society, we live with a system where success is rewarded with more money. But in these surveys, the experts have found that money is well down the list of motivating factors.

A unique effort

One thing that motivates employees to higher levels of production and proficiency is recognition. In a world crowded with millions of people, they want to know that what they do as individuals can make a difference and that their work and effort can set them apart from the crowd as being unique.

We have great examples of how motivation can work in both team and individual areas when we look at college football. Numerous teams have a system in place that acknowledges both team success and individual achievement. In most years, teams like Ohio State, Michigan, and Florida State are contenders for bowl games and national championships. The goal of team success is to be invited to a bowl and possibly win a national championship. But these teams offer recognition to individuals who make significant contributions to the team goal by awarding stickers for their helmets. During team meetings after a game, the coaches award a player a buckeye leaf, a gold football, or a tomahawk that will be stuck on the helmet for the next week's game.

By the end of the season, a player can nearly cover his helmet with these awards. So the player is recognized in front of teammates and gains recognition for his contributions to the success of the team by displaying his awards throughout the year to the fans.

Knowing that recognition is important, a boss must use this principle to motivate employees. Positive reinforcement and recognition should become regular and exciting for employees. The question is how to do it. There are many ways to offer recognition; it just takes a little imagination. It also takes discipline. Recognition is not something that can be done sporadically and achieve the desired result.

A program

You can set up an employee of the week or employee of the month program. If someone has excelled for a specific period of time, grant a special parking place, a small prize, or some other special privilege for an allotted amount of time. Hold a special meeting of all employees to award employees who have excelled.

A public place

To make this recognition stick longer, find ways to post the names of those who have won the awards. If you have an employee of the month award, display the picture in a place of prominence. Buy a plaque that lists the names of other winners. You can purchase plaques that have places for twelve winners. In this way you will be able to give public recognition to an employee for an extended period of time.

And visitors, vendors, workers from other areas of the company, and executives from other parts of the building will be able to see the achievements of your workers and congratulate them.

A caution

Some words of caution here. Be consistent in making these awards. Do not expect one or two months to make all the difference you hope it will. Also, as you continue to make the awards, make the standards move up gradually. Finally, don't feel that everyone in the area must receive the award. An award for extraordinary work is just that, not a rotating award until everyone has a chance.

CHAPTER 21

Build jobs around employees' strengths

You want to work with employees to get them to strengthen their weaknesses. But don't make the fatal mistake of focusing on their weaknesses. Find ways to reorganize the jobs so that each employee is doing work in an area of strength. But don't take away any challenges for the employee to grow.

A chance to blossom

Let's face facts. No one wants to be in a position of doing something hated and constantly facing failure or the chance for reprimand for a substandard job. If you give employees the chance to do what they like and to use their gifts, they will begin to blossom. They will be motivated to pay you back by making you look good.

It takes work to get things organized in a way that employees can spend the majority of time focusing on tasks that they can do well. If they believe that they are encouraged to grow but have the chance to work in areas of strength, they will work harder at shoring up areas where they fall short, and they will continue to produce excellent work in general for you.

A chance to succeed

Another thing happens when you give employees jobs that allow them to exercise their gifts regularly: they get excited about doing their jobs. They know that they will be able to accomplish lots of things, and so they are excited about coming to work and succeeding. And that is the goal of a great boss: to create an environment for employees where they can succeed.

That doesn't mean employees will have jobs that allow them to do only what they like to do. Each employee will still need to be challenged to grow, to stretch, and to improve. But if they know that they are being set up to win, they will be much more willing to work at things that they don't do well.

As with any idea to motivate employees, you need to be clear with them why you are doing the things you do, to encourage them to achieve, and to let them know that you believe in them. It is your job to create an environment where people can be successful. So the challenge of creating jobs around the strengths of your employees is not just a nice thing to do; it is crucial to the success you want to have in your job.

CHAPTER 22

Give credit where credit is due

*N*othing is more demoralizing to an employee than to work hard and accomplish something and not get the credit or to have the credit go to another person. This is especially important to remember as you manage groups of people.

What happens when you report employees' ideas and subsequent successes, but you take the credit, or you dilute the praise by giving credit always to the whole group? You rob employees of a chance to make their mark, you rob them of recognition that they have earned, and you rob them of any incentive for doing remarkable things.

Report to executives

When you have the chance to report to executives on the area you are managing, point out persons who did or are doing an excellent job, came up with a great idea, or made the big sale. Their success will only reflect on what a great job you must be doing as a manager.

Your success depends entirely on the job done by your employees. It is to your advantage to give credit to those who have done the work.

Tell employees

Another aspect of this principle is that you must let employees know when they have done excellent jobs. Telling your superiors where credit is due is just half of your job. Letting those employees know how well they are doing is the other half, especially when some employees try to take credit for things that they didn't really do. You know these employees. Some employees always seem to be around excellent work and take credit for everything that was done. If they contributed, give them credit for their part. But if they just happened to be around or pushed their way in for credit, be sure to give the credit to people who really did the work or made the contribution.

Address teams

When you have people working in teams or groups, recognize the entire group as well as individuals. You need to motivate people to work together; foster an attitude of teamwork by crediting everyone who had a part.

The basis of giving credit to the right people for the right things is knowing what people are doing. Be aware of who is assigned to a project, and be involved so that you can see who is doing the work. This takes effort on your part, but it will yield great results.

CHAPTER 23

Program small victories

*I*n many companies, the management staff looks for the person who is able, on occasion, to deliver the big deal or have an amazingly innovative idea. These people are valuable. Don't misunderstand. But the law of averages dictates that most employees who work for you will not be this kind of worker.

All winners

The majority of workers you will manage will be people who come to work, want to do a good job, and then want to go home. If you are to motivate these people beyond this concept of a job, you must help them feel and understand how exciting it can be to be a part of a cutting edge, winning team. And there is only one way that anyone can know what it feels like to be a part of a winning team: have some victories.

To help your team get that infectious love of winning, create situations where each employee can win consistently. We are not talking about a million-dollar sale or an idea for a new product that will earn your company millions of dollars. We are talking about finding a way that each employee can contribute to the bottom line.

A winning example

Perhaps you have an employee in your mail room who just puts in his time. Your postage costs are rising quickly and exerting a lot of pressure on your budget. You happen to know of a bulk mailing service that will allow your company to save more than 15 percent on postage costs. Should you call this company and make a deal? Perhaps. But it is also a perfect situation for you to give the name of the company and the contact there, along with several other companies to contact, to this employee to research. Help him understand what kinds of answers you need. Meet regularly with the employee doing the research to review his progress in finding a better method to handle the mail.

The bottom line is this: by helping an employee do this work instead of getting on the phone yourself and making a deal, you're creating a victory opportunity for this employee. He will have the chance to contact people outside the company, learn how to do research, ask questions, and make a recommendation to you about what company can save you the most money and offer you the best service. And when it is all said and done, he has had an active part in saving your company money.

CHAPTER 24

Listen to what
your employees mean

*F*or a manager, it is essential to speak with truth, integrity, and honesty. And it is no less essential to learn how to listen effectively.

Communication can break down in two major areas. The first is being articulate enough to say exactly what you mean or to clearly explain how you feel. The second is taking the verbal communication that comes from another person and deciphering it correctly. With two problem areas and two people involved, that means four areas are vulnerable to breakdown.

Listen

The first step in understanding what your employees mean is simply listening. Far too often, managers (and people in general) want to quickly respond to something that was said. Hold that impulse, and let the other person speak. Perhaps the other person becomes quiet for a few moments; let the silence work. Maybe what the other person wants to say is all jumbled up inside, and it takes some time to come out. Perhaps the person is feeling very emotional about the subject. Don't rush the person.

Ask questions

Once employees have said what is on their minds, ask some questions that will help you understand better. Learn to identify a hidden meaning in what they are saying or how they are saying it.

When one employee is hurt or frustrated, he will often respond to a discussion of the situation by saying, "I just don't care anymore." At face value, it's a worrisome remark. How can you motivate an employee who has no interest in his job anymore?

But with the proper questions, it becomes obvious that what is behind this statement is hurt. Perhaps he feels that his work isn't being recognized, perhaps something was said that demeaned him, and just maybe he is misinterpreting something, making it a personal issue when it is a professional issue.

By saying that he doesn't care, he is trying to distance himself from being hurt anymore. If he doesn't care, no one can hurt him. Obviously, dealing with an employee who truly doesn't care is very different from dealing with an employee who perhaps cares too much.

When a manager listens to what this employee means, she is able to work on the real issue. Had the manager not gotten to the real meaning of the employee's statements, both would be frustrated.

Clarify the issue

Clarify what your employees mean. "Do you mean this, or do you mean that?" is a great starter. "You sound angry, but are you disappointed or hurt and it is coming out in anger?" is another good one.

Listen, think about what is being said, and ask questions. You will see improvements in your communication with your employees.

CHAPTER 25

Become an advocate

As a boss, you are only as good as the people who work for you. No matter what you do, if they don't do their jobs, you don't look like you are doing a good job. So one of the chores that falls to you as a boss is to make sure employees get credit for doing their jobs as well as they do them.

Plead the case

Being an advocate means that one person pleads the case of another person. As a boss, you should be performing this very basic duty. Being an advocate doesn't mean that you talk only about all of the good things that an employee does, although that is certainly a big part of it. It also means that you come to the defense of your employees when they do something wrong or unacceptable within your company.

If you want employees to have the power to do their jobs, make decisions on their own, and take control of their work, you have to accept the fact that they're going to make mistakes. As an advocate, you have the job of protecting them and defending their actions (we are not talking here of cheating, lying, stealing, or other character offenses). When they make a decision that was well intentioned but wrong, your job is to point out why what they did was wrong, try to correct it, and defend employees to anyone who is critical or deprecating.

No one likes mistakes. But everyone makes them. So as an advocate, you are to plead the cause, the abilities, and the rationale of the employee. Take the heat.

When employees know that you are not just encouraging them to take chances, but you are defending their right to do so as well as their right to make mistakes, they will become motivated to do the best job possible.

Be a faithful spokesperson

To be an advocate, through success and through failure, will allow employees to know that you truly believe in their abilities and that you have faith in their commitment to get the job done. Being an active supporter of employees is a powerful motivator.

CHAPTER 26

Don't make promises you can't keep

*T*here are two specific reasons not to make promises to employees that you cannot or do not intend to keep. First, if you can't keep a promise that you have made, you seriously erode the trust factor. When trust is eroded, the relationship deteriorates. When a relationship begins to deteriorate, management becomes very difficult if possible at all. Second, as a boss, if you make promises to an employee that you don't honor, you can be held legally liable. The legal concept is called *promissory estoppel*.

Do unto others . . .

First, the trust issue. A bit of role reversal is the easiest way to illustrate why broken promises are so harmful. Imagine you are sitting with your boss or a client. The person makes a promise to you that you accept as credible. But as time goes on, you find that the person can't or won't honor the commitment made to you. What is your response? Probably you feel hurt, unmotivated to help this person, and maybe even a little vindictive. You may decide that you don't want to do business with the person again. Over time you may learn to live with it, but things can probably never be the same again.

When you turn the tables and you become the boss, you can see where you can easily create sour attitudes and perhaps cause good people to leave your employ if you aren't careful about the commitments you make. This whole issue boils down to this principle: do unto others as you would have them do unto you.

Guard your guarantees

Regarding the principle of promissory estoppel, things can get very sticky. If you tell an employee that you are going to make sure she gets a specific job but then for whatever reason she doesn't get that job, you can be held legally liable as a boss for making a promise that you didn't keep. Penalties can vary; you may be forced to put that person in the job, and financial penalties may be assessed. In talking about the future of an employee, never make specific promises or implied promises about things that you cannot control or that you might change your mind about.

The whole basis of a concept like promissory estoppel is based on one thing—fairness. Making promises that you can't or won't keep just isn't fair.

CHAPTER 27

Be a servant

*P*robably every one of us grew up with the idea that bosses had the power to delegate all the jobs they didn't like doing to others who had to do their bidding. Well, that *may* have been true then (although it's not likely), but it certainly isn't true now. In today's environment as a leader, you are to be a servant to those who work for you. You are to serve them, create an atmosphere where they can win, and care about them as people.

But what exactly does it mean to be a servant? A person functions as a servant by performing services for another. How does being a boss begin to figure into this definition?

Deter distractions

Quite easily. Look at a corporation as an organism. Each person plays a role in maintaining the health of that organism. Each person performs duties that keep everything running smoothly. A boss's duty or function is to be sure that employees have every opportunity to perform their functions as well as possible. To serve your employees means to provide leadership, training, tools, and an atmosphere where they can concentrate on their jobs and their performance without worrying about distractions that take their focus away from what they were hired to do.

Equip employees

To be a servant means to shape budgets to be sure that there is enough money to train your employees adequately. You help set goals so your employees can know how well they are doing. Through the corporate system, you obtain new or better equipment that will make your employees more productive. You set the tone, values, and attitude of your workplace so that it is a place of motivation, positive reinforcement, and growth and development of your employees.

If you are a servant and look out for the needs of your employees adequately, you will have fulfilled a large part of your function as a boss. No one employee can perform every function in a company. Your function as a boss is to equip and lead a group of people.

Set the pace

Being a servant in the workplace is often misunderstood as taking the commands of those who work for you. Nothing could be further from the truth. You need to hear what your employees need and want. But you are not at their beck and call. You are to set the pace so that they can perform at a high level and feel good about their accomplishments. A servant boss will look for every inhibitor to great performance and attack it with passion, understanding, and a desire to create an environment where employees can excel.

If you are a servant in these ways, people you serve will rise to new levels of productivity and self-esteem because they will be able to concentrate on what they do.

CHAPTER 28

Quantify all jobs

*E*very company has jobs that are easily measured. But many jobs require creativity to measure their productivity.

Accuracy as a goal

In the shipping department of a major clothes chain, there was a large sign that stated, "100 Percent Accuracy Is Our Goal." Next to the slogan was a sign that declared how many packages had been shipped since the last mistake was made. The goal was clear, and the company recognized the need to celebrate the hard work the packagers were investing in reaching their goal. It also showed them when they had made a mistake and had to start over at meeting their goal.

Objective measures

While it is not good for the company to have nebulously defined jobs, it is equally damaging for the employees. The measure of their work's effectiveness becomes less objective with fewer concrete expectations. If your employees don't know what you expect of them, how can you give awards for doing a great job or hold them responsible for falling short of expectations?

Some jobs lend themselves quite easily to objective standards. Salespeople can be held accountable for the dollar value of their sales or the number of new accounts they bring in or the number of contacts that they make in a month. Service people can be held accountable for the number of successful situations handled without a callback. People involved in filling orders or shipping products can be measured by how many correct orders they fill or ship without a return.

Creative measures

But other jobs are more difficult to measure. How do you measure the productivity of a public relations person? How do you measure the productivity of human resources people who are charged with getting the best people put into positions within the company? What about a computer programmer? Often, there are no easy answers. It is possible, though, to quantify almost every job.

Let's look at a computer programmer as an example. A programmer is charged with creating programs that service a need within the organization. Because of the complex technical knowledge needed to program a computer, the standards for a programmer are often avoided. Maybe you measure the number of lines of computer code that a programmer writes in a day or averages per day over a week. Maybe you measure the number of programs written that are free from bugs, or you measure the number of bugs present in a program. There are numerous ways to measure productivity.

In setting these kinds of measures, you do well to involve your employees in discussions about how they should be measured. They often know more about their jobs than you do, and they can be great sources of insight when deciding on the types of performance measurements you should use.

CHAPTER 29

Create
positive momentum

*E*very boss has had employees who, for some reason, are having a hard time in getting things going positively in their direction. Perhaps they took part in a project that didn't go well, maybe they worked under another manager who demotivated employees, or maybe they lack the self-confidence to perform to the level of their abilities. Regardless of the reason, you need to work with them and get them back on track.

On the right track

They need to get back on track to being the productive employees that they can become, and they need to get back on track for their personal development. If someone doesn't help them, they may never be the persons they could be. There is only one way for them to get straightened out: to have a victory and begin to believe in their abilities.

As a manager, whether you believe that it is your responsibility to help these people or not, you are likely to be the one to pull them from the wreckage of their past and set them on a course to success. Having inherited this task, you have only one place to begin: at the beginning.

Spend some time with these employees, and find out what

makes them tick. Do some of the other things that we have talked about, including evaluating their talents and their likes and dislikes. Analyze the jobs that you are asking them to perform. Develop plans that will begin to build their confidence.

On the job

When working on job descriptions with these employees, program in duties that they will be able to perform well. Don't try to stretch them too far too soon. Meet regularly with them, and talk about what they are doing, what things are going well, and what things are hanging them up. Encourage them to try, support them in their efforts, and work with them to avoid failure early on.

If you can develop jobs that will help your company and give the employees the opportunity to rebuild their confidence and enthusiasm, you will have gone a long way toward restoring their dignity and self-worth. And it is quite possible that you will find some of your best employees this way.

On their own

In programming a series of small victories for these employees, don't make the mistake of not holding them accountable or of getting so involved that you don't let them do the work. If you do it for them and they succeed, you have accomplished nothing. They must succeed on their own abilities. You can aid, support, and encourage, but you can't do the work for them.

Once they have succeeded, you can begin to stretch them, allowing them to build or rebuild their confidence in their talents. It is a gradual process. It takes time and commitment to program employees for victory. But that is what your job is all about: creating an environment where employees can excel and be productive for the company.

CHAPTER 30

Lead by example

*I*f you want your employees to behave in a certain way, it is imperative that you behave in that way, too. If it is important to you that your employees present a certain image, you must present that image, too. If on your team you expect anyone who sees work that needs to be done to do it, you can't avoid doing work that you find, either.

Determine the direction

Leadership means that you are at the front of the pack, setting the pace and determining the direction. If you are angry all the time, you can expect anger in employees. If you are ready to work with a positive attitude, you will see that exhibited in your employees. If you want employees to show up for work early, show up early. If you want employees who will willingly stay until the work for the day is done, you had better be prepared to stay. You may never see your traits in your employees to the same extent that you exhibit them, but they will be present in some form or another.

So it follows that if you want to have happy, highly motivated employees, you better learn to exhibit happy, highly motivated traits in your work life. You cannot expect what you cannot display yourself. That is what is so essential about leadership.

Recall principles

Leading by example really goes back to the basic principles you want to run your business by. You must go back to the principles and compare them to what you are displaying by your behavior. All too often, it is easy to expect one thing and live another. We all do it.

When you recognize inconsistencies, try to narrow the gap between expectations and behavior. When you fall short, admit it. Pride is perhaps the most negative quality that you can exhibit when trying to motivate your employees. If you seem too good to live up to your own standards, those who work for you will have no motivation to live up to them, either.

CHAPTER 31

Create incentives

M any companies believe that the best way to motivate employees is to pay them. If you pay them enough for the job and give them raises when they have earned them, management is doing everything possible to motivate employees. Nothing could be further from the truth, however.

In many studies of motivation—and specifically related to what employees say about it—money is well down the list. Money does have importance, but most employees place recognition at the top of the list. Recognition is a benefit that allows self-esteem to grow. Let's face it. All employees want to feel good about themselves.

Clear reward

So, one positive way to motivate your employees to do exceptional work is to create incentives that will allow them to have a clear reward they can strive for. For example, many organizations offer cash bonuses for certain levels of productivity.

The form of the incentive is really less important than the fact that some type of incentive is in place. Incentives can be very simple to complex. They range from naming an employee of the week all the way to awarding corporate titles that allow each employee to be honored both inside and outside of the corporation.

Each company has a different corporate culture and idea of appropriate incentives. You will have to be creative within your company to develop incentive plans. You can designate a parking place for the employee of the week or month. You can throw a little party each month to recognize employees who have excelled. You can award cash bonuses to employees for specific accomplishments that save the company money. Let your imagination run wild. Incentives don't have to be elaborate or costly. The recognition of work done well counts for more than the value of the award.

Specific reward

A restaurant well known for its food and its service had a program of honoring the employee of the month. Management would reward employees who went above and beyond the call of duty in offering service by naming one employee every month; the employee's name was inscribed on a plaque that hung in the foyer of the building. Nearly every employee strove to get the name on the plaque. At the end of each year, the person who had been mentioned most often got to keep the plaque permanently.

Obviously, it is easier to create an incentive when you have clear, concrete goals for each job, such as doing whatever it takes to make a customer happy. Then incentives are moved from the subjective (who is easy to get along with and who talks about accomplishments more) to a very objective standard that everyone knows. The more concrete the job descriptions and goals, the easier it will be to create incentives.

CHAPTER 32

Praise employees publicly

As many studies have shown, recognition is one of the most highly motivating factors to employees. If you truly understand this concept, you will understand that appropriate praise for work well done is not something that should be meted out on a meager scale.

The office

If you are having regular meetings with your employees on an individual basis, you will have the opportunity to let them know the areas that they are excelling in as well as the areas that they need to give more attention to. This approach helps you build a good relationship with all employees who report to you. But there is a great need to take your praise out of your office and into the workplace.

The workplace

When employees do a great job, let them know it in front of their peers. This praise will build the esteem of the employees who do good work. The other employees who desire to have the same kind of recognition will work harder and look for things to do that will get you to praise them publicly.

You know how you feel when you are praised openly for your accomplishments. Don't be selfish with the feeling. Work it in as an integral part of your work routine.

The "star"

This principle can get you into real trouble if you apply your praise in an unfair way. Every manager has at one time or another had a star employee who seems to do everything well. Publicly praising that employee for everything worthy of mention will quite possibly work against you by creating animosity between that person and the peers. It can also lead to the assumption that you are playing favorites and that no one else can reach the standard set by the "star." Both results may motivate one employee while demotivating others, and in either case, public praise for the work of your employees has backfired and created a disincentive for others.

Praise and recognition are very powerful tools. But using them incorrectly can create more problems. Be judicious in your use of praise, but don't be stingy.

CHAPTER 33

Make all responsibilities concrete

When you have something that needs to be done, it is incumbent on you as a supervisor to be sure that employees understand exactly what they are being required to do. A vague conversation leaves lots of opportunity for misunderstanding and miscommunication.

We have talked about the need to define each job in a job description so that employees know exactly what they are supposed to do. The same principle is at work when you make individual assignments.

Here's the idea

I did some work once for a man I had known for some time. We had a long discussion about the tasks he wanted to hire me to perform. During the meeting, he took what I thought were extensive notes. When the meeting was finished, he took an extra five minutes to review every task we had discussed and the amount he was agreeing to pay, and he gave me an exact date to have the work completed. I then had an easy job in writing up an agreement. Every detail—the job, the price, and the deadline—was clearly laid out. No other person had been that explicit with me before. It worked so well that I have tried to incorporate this technique in my management.

Here's the approach

Suppose you tell an employee to do some research and turn in a report about the challenges to be faced over the next five years. If you make the assignment and say nothing more than what is contained in the first sentence of this paragraph, odds are that the report will be too brief or too long. Quite possibly, the employee may research a number of things that you didn't necessarily want included, or he may leave out entire areas that you felt were important. After you see the report, you instruct him to go back and rework the material and possibly do additional work; you aren't happy with the initial efforts. The employee can easily become frustrated, feeling he has failed you.

You significantly reduce the chances for miscommunication by saying, "I need a ten-page report on the challenges of the next five years. I want you to cover sales, manufacturing, the impact of technology, budget, and personnel. I need you to have this finished on December 15."

That doesn't mean you won't think of additional things to include after you have seen the report. The employee's work may very well spur your thinking, and you will need further research on a topic. But she knows she delivered exactly what you were expecting. When an employee is clear on this point, she can succeed by providing you exactly what you asked for.

This approach will also lower anxiety for both you and your employee. You won't wonder what in the world he is working on. He won't be working under a cloud of doubt that no matter what he does, you won't be happy.

Here's practice

A good exercise to practice is to write out the specifics of each assignment. Give a copy to the employee, and keep one for yourself. This discipline will help you be sure that you have communicated what you wanted.

CHAPTER 34

Set firm deadlines

O ne great pitfall of communicating details of assignments or asking for certain types of work to be done is neglecting to set firm deadlines. You fail to tell employees when you would like to have the project completed. It may be an oversight on your part, you may not even be sure when you need something done, or you may assume that they know when it must be done, so the deadline is fuzzy or not stated finally and clearly.

Avert frustration

This fuzziness can create an enormous amount of frustration for you and your employees. If they know that something is important and needs to be done by Friday, they generally will get it done by Friday. If you communicate to your employees that they need to get something done but fail to clearly say when, they will unconsciously put a lower priority on the work. However, if you are specific and clear about the work, they will plan other things around it to be sure that it is done.

Sometimes as a boss, you may feel that you have been very clear, and then you get upset when they haven't gotten work done in the proper time. The employees claim that you never told them when the work had to be done. You can engage in a simple exercise that will significantly enhance your communication as well as give you a fallback to make sure that you did set a deadline.

Use a form

Develop a form that will take, at most, one minute to fill out. List the project, the name of the employee, the date the assignment was given, the date the work is due to be completed, and any specific requirements that you may have for that project. When you talk with an employee about the assignment, fill out the form, sign it, have her sign it, and then make a copy of it for her files. Keep your copy in a file for that employee so that whenever you meet with her, you can go over the projects she is currently working on.

Usually, you won't need to fill out a form for every assignment. In fact, after you get in the habit of filling out the form, you may find that you have improved your communication enough to stop using it. But be careful not to stop before you have firmly established the habit of communicating firm deadlines for work you assign.

CHAPTER 35

Know when not to say anything

*J*ust as there are many styles of bosses, there are many styles of employees. You need to constantly push and encourage some employees to go farther, work harder, and accomplish more. But other employees are highly motivated and have higher standards for themselves than you would ever feel comfortable setting for them.

People perception

This is truly one of the most challenging aspects of being a manager. You must be able to read the people who work for you and know what they need in specific instances. Giving too much leeway to an employee who needs more structure is inviting disaster. Being too firm or aggressive with an employee who already is driven to succeed and has very high standards is running the very real risk of making that employee feel that he has little value and that you don't trust him, both of which will lead to a lack of motivation, at least in the short term.

In dealing with the latter kind of employee, you must recognize that when she has made a mistake or allowed something to go astray, she doesn't need you to drive the point home. She needs you to point out the problem and let her deal with it. You don't excuse what she has done; you don't let things slide. But you deal with each person as an individual.

To be sure, you will make mistakes, especially when you are just beginning in a new area with new employees or when you hire or promote new people into your area. Confronting an employee with work that falls short of your expectations is a necessity. How far and how hard to press the point require the art of management.

Coaching, not encroaching

The coach of a sports team must constantly motivate some players because they lack the internal discipline to do it themselves. The coach must prod them to live up to their potential. But many players work harder than others because of their internal drive and motivation. The latter kind of player can be a leader, an inspiration to other players, and needs only to be aimed in the right direction.

If Wayne Gretzky ("the great one"), now the highest scoring hockey player in history, makes a mistake on the ice, his coach doesn't scream at him or pull him from the game. The coach knows that Gretzky's desire to excel is so high that any extra negative pressure runs the risk of demotivating him. Instead, the coach may give some direction about what Gretzky may want to do the next time he is in such a situation.

No formulas

An old proverb says there is nothing as unequal as treating unequal people equally. Although it may be easier for you as a manager to treat all employees the same, recognize that they are not. You are paid to create a winning team, not to have a formula for dealing with those who work for you.

CHAPTER 36

Respect time

As a boss, you can identify things that you wish were different for you and your boss and correct them with the people who work for you. And many bosses fail to respect the time of their employees.

A frustration maker

A leader of one small company is oblivious to time. His first meeting of the day usually starts on time. But if things get involved, its ending time or the beginning of his next meeting is delayed. Although the person he is meeting with feels good because of the extra attention, the other people scheduled for meetings get frustrated, believing that their issues are less important. Employees always make a great effort to schedule a meeting early in the day to be sure they get the time they need with this leader.

To have good communication, you schedule regular meetings with the people who work for you. You have many other meetings as well. There is nothing so demotivating as a boss showing (not telling) an employee that his time is less valuable than someone else's.

Punctuality

When you schedule a meeting with an employee for 2:00, be there ready to start the meeting at 2:00. If you are busy doing other things or caught up in a meeting with someone else and can't begin until 2:30, 2:45, or even 3:00, you are not respecting the time of the employee. Employees have other tasks than being available to you when you are finally ready to give them some of your time.

Commitment

Making an appointment is making a commitment. Live up to your commitments. Show each employee the value of living up to personal commitments.

Professionalism

By being on time, starting and stopping meetings at agreed-upon times, you will deal with things in a more timely and professional manner. Things won't get bogged down with unnecessary delays because meetings are always running late or being put off because you can't honor the time of employees.

Effectiveness

When you schedule adequate time with a designated end, time will be used more effectively. By honoring time commitments, you must give those who work for you enough time but not so much that they take your time for granted. Beginning and ending meetings on time, if you aren't already doing that, will come as a shock to everyone. Hang in there. Soon, the system will adjust itself, and things will begin to run more smoothly. Everyone will have more time to get things done, and meetings won't become meandering organisms with lives of their own.

Create an atmosphere where people can be motivated and get things done. Respecting others' time shows you respect your time. Begin to get yourself on a schedule to respect those who work for you.

DEVELOPMENT

CHAPTER 37

Focus on strengths

*T*o help your employees grow to their full potential, maintain the perspective that they have been gifted in specific ways. Every person has certain strengths and certain weaknesses.

Recognize gifts

As you try to help employees excel, you need to discover their weaknesses and recognize that they probably will not ever excel in these areas. People will naturally be drawn to things that they do well. They will avoid tasks that are more difficult for them.

As a boss, you want them to become more rounded, but you also want them to perform at a very high level. The reality is that employees will never perform at a high level if they are focused *only* on tasks that highlight their weaknesses.

Do you want a person to spend too large a part of time working at less than maximum efficiency? Of course not.

So when developing job descriptions for people, you ought to give them enough tasks that they are equipped to do well. No job, for anyone, focuses entirely on the things that the employee is good at or likes well, but you are defeating yourself by not giving an employee a job that plays to strengths.

Restructure

Sometimes you may have to reorganize tasks in an area. Sometimes you may have to move people to different areas. Sometimes you may have to remove a person who really has no abilities in a given area.

Reorganizing to fit the strengths of your people may meet with resistance in your organization. Leaders may have had a certain structure for quite some time. So you will have to do some politicking to get the freedom to make the moves that you believe will make your area more effective.

Moving people to new positions can be a boon to the individuals, the manager, and the organization. It simply makes no sense for anyone to keep people in jobs they are not equipped for.

Reevaluate

Termination is not something to be taken lightly. But if a person refuses to move to another area and simply cannot perform the functions the job requires, termination allows the company the opportunity to fill the position with a more effective employee and allows the terminated employee to be removed from the pressure of performing that particular job. The terminated employee can then look for positions that are a better fit for his or her skills.

It will take time to make all the moves necessary to get the most effective alignment of people. It is not something to rush, and every move should be evaluated carefully before making it, complete with plenty of input from employees. But once you have people placed in jobs that play to their strengths, the productivity of your employees will be higher than you ever thought possible.

CHAPTER 38

Create specific standards of performance

*T*rying to excel or achieve at a job without a specific plan impairs employees. It is tough to live up to unknown or unspoken standards. So to have your employees reach beyond their current levels, set specific goals for them in each area of responsibility.

Each job under your management should have a clear and acceptable job description written for it. This guide explains what the job entails and the tasks you wish to have done. But a job description is general. To help your employees grow, you will need to make standards of performance as specific as you can.

Realistic goals

Sit down with your employee and find out exactly what she feels she can accomplish in the next year. (Often employees will feel that they can achieve more than you would ask them to.) Let her set her sights high, but don't let her set unrealistic goals. Once you have come up with these measurable goals, write them down, and both you and the employee sign the list. It should be binding—unless at a later time you both agree that new circumstances have altered either side's ability to live by the agreement.

Reassuring goals

One company prepared job descriptions but didn't clearly define what was expected in terms of results. About two years later, it instituted a program with clear standards of performance, stating what was expected to be accomplished at the end of the year. That year of having a clear understanding of performance goals was distinctly different from the previous years. Employees excelled at tasks and surpassed them in several areas. There was less stress or anxiety for them. They knew what was expected and what kind of progress they were making. When their annual reviews rolled around, they were excited, knowing that they had succeeded in doing their jobs.

Quantifiable goals

In almost every job there is a way to set specific, quantifiable goals for an employee. If a person works in shipping, one goal could be the number of shipments that he packs without an error. Another goal could be the average number of packages shipped in a day.

But there are jobs where specific goals can be more difficult. Take, for example, a marketing job. Nearly every organization has specific sales goals that need to be met weekly, monthly, quarterly, and yearly. But they have a marketing team that has the responsibility to make the company recognizable and to give products a high profile. But there are few ways the effectiveness of their ads can be measured. On the other hand, direct marketers measure the effectiveness of every ad or mailing. Finding ways to bring accountability to activities is fundamental to standards of performance.

This kind of goal setting helps you develop more rounded employees. You have salespeople who are bringing back the sales and also developing future business. And if they meet both goals that you set with them, you can significantly increase the level of productivity for them the next year.

However, the most important thing about setting these goals with your employees is that they know exactly what they must do to successfully complete their jobs. And in most cases, people will work very hard, will work extra hours, and will do whatever they have to do to meet their standards of performance.

Motivating goals

With this tool, you can make management a much easier task. Employees will know what they are supposed to be doing. The target for employees isn't moving with the day-to-day changes in the environment. They can set their sights and act accordingly. And best of all, they experience a feeling of deep satisfaction when they can go into an end-of-the-year review knowing full well that they have done the job. They will be encouraged to continue to set higher goals so that they can challenge themselves to higher levels of achievement.

CHAPTER 39

Recognize your most important investment

*I*n helping employees develop their skills and abilities, you can give them one commodity that is invaluable. And only you can give it to them: YOUR time. Giving time to employees is giving them a sense that they are important, that they have worth, and that you value them and their contributions.

When you talk to busy people about how they find time for their children, they will often respond something like this: "I am very busy, but I make sure that I spend quality time with my kids since I can't spend quantities of time with them."

Quality and quantity

Don't fall into the trap of believing this myth. Kids need to have quality time and quantities of time. Quantity of time instills in them a sense of value that even high-quality time can't. While managing workers is different from raising a family, the principle is the same. Employees can gain a sense of personal value if they are worthy of time with their supervisor.

Managers are stretched to complete all the tasks they are responsible for in the eight hours that they have each day.

They must wrangle with budgets, equipment problems, and personnel problems, plan, review the statistics of their areas, and spend time with employees. But ignoring the employees is shortsighted and ultimately disabling to employees and managers.

Schedule time with every person who reports to you. In this formal time you can review progress on job issues, such as production, efficiency, personnel problems, and personal development. But just as essential is the informal time that you are able to create to be with your employees.

This informal time is what Tom Peters (author of *A Passion for Excellence*) calls *management by walking around*. Walk around the areas of people you supervise. Ask them questions about what you see. Find out what they are working on. You can even take a little time to see how they are doing personally: spouses or kids, school sports or other local activities. These casual moments inform your employees that you care about them as people as well as care about what they can do for you.

Schedule this time into your calendar. Take one hour a week to make the rounds. You don't always have to take this walk at the same time or on the same day. Fit it into your schedule when you can. But fit it in. Catch your employees doing their jobs. Let them know that you do care. Care is contagious. The more you care for them, the more they will care about you and their jobs.

CHAPTER 40

Evaluate regularly

*O*nce you have instituted the practice of creating a specific standard of performance for each employee, your work has only begun. The standard of performance is worth little if it is not followed up regularly with meetings to measure how progress toward goals is moving.

Avert surprises

These evaluations serve at least two purposes. First, they prevent you as a manager from being surprised if things changed during the year and things weren't going as you agreed at the beginning of the year. Second, they keep employees focused on exactly what you want to accomplish in a year. It is amazing how many things can creep into a job and eat up valuable time in twelve short months. To avoid surprises, regular evaluations are critical.

But remember, a standard of performance is a plan. It is a plan agreed to by both you and the employee. You should stick to the plan tenaciously. Hold the employee accountable for what she agreed to do in a given period. But use the plan as a motivator, not a means of punishment.

Like any plan, it can be changed. Things happen in a year

that can drastically change an employee's ability to fulfill his part of an agreement with you. If, for instance, he agreed to keep costs of manufacturing a product at a certain level, there are only so many factors that he can control. Perhaps one material, such as oil, suddenly increases in price by 50 percent. You should challenge him to meet the goals you agreed on. But if at the end of the year the price of manufacturing has been reduced except for that uncontrollable spike in oil prices, you need to recognize that he did everything in his power to keep that production cost in line. In fact, he met the goal to the best of his ability.

Learn

Use these events as learning experiences. Better planning the next year can take into account possible fluctuations or build in contingencies for unexpected events.

But the value of the standards of performance is having a firm plan and goal in mind. Everyone knows what is expected.

Focus on improvement

Many jobs are hard to quantify. You probably can't ask a computer programmer to finish twenty-eight projects. You have no way of knowing how involved these projects might be. But you can set a standard that at the end of the year, the programmer will have written an average of 250 lines of computer code for every workday. This approach allows the programmer flexibility in the short term but a definite goal in the long term. If you meet with your programmers monthly, they can evaluate with you if they are on a pace to average that much production. They can pick up the pace or find ways to improve their productivity.

Regular meetings keep everyone informed about how

things are going and let employees know that they are responsible for their own work behavior. They stay focused. And you have the chance to praise their work if they are completing the tasks you have asked them to complete.

Employees live with some degree of uncertainty that they are not performing something correctly. Regular evaluation allows them the freedom to know how they are doing and to go on with the encouragement of their supervisor.

CHAPTER 41

Develop a vision

*J*ust as you plan the work you have to do as a manager, you must plan for the development of the people who work for you. You may have a clear-cut program to develop your staff. Your company may have training programs that you can encourage your employees to enroll in. Or you may have to put considerable time and effort into developing a program to give your employees more skills, boosting their self-esteem as well as making them more valued employees.

Be supportive

If you have established programs for training and continuing education, you must encourage your employees to take advantage of them, and you must support them as they try to learn. Nearly all training will involve a commitment of time. Cheerfully give them the time. If you complain about lost productivity in the short run, you will discourage employees from pursuing opportunities available to them.

If you don't have a clear program, take some time to think about each employee. For each person, list strengths and weaknesses. Talk with employees about what you see as their strengths and weaknesses, and find out what kinds of work excite them. Reflect on all your observations and the information that they give you. What areas in the company can they grow into? What level of responsibility do they want to achieve? Are appropriate learning opportunities available?

You should find out your company's plans for the future. Which skills will be needed? Are more technical jobs going to open up? Is the company going to expand its lines of products? Would some of your employees be suitable for advanced training in these areas?

Be aware

For some training, you will need to know the education requirements. Is there a degree that will help employees? Is there a college or university nearby? Have you learned of seminars and professional training? If you are like most managers, you are deluged with seminar advertisements. If you don't find what you are looking for, write the seminar company describing your needs.

Be challenging

Analyze the training you can offer them. Can you come alongside them and allow them to learn new jobs? Institute a program where employees learn to do the jobs of others in their area. The more employees know how their jobs affect other areas, the more likely they will be to complete their jobs appropriately, and the better they will be able to develop ideas that will save time, money, and effort.

Begin as soon as you can. Set some time aside to think about the employees who report to you. Reflect on strengths and weaknesses, and begin to imagine where they can go in your company and how they can grow and realize their potential. The closer they come to realizing their potential, the more valuable they will be to you and to your company.

CHAPTER 42

Budget money for continuing education

*A*fter you have developed a plan for each person who works for you, implement it. Implementation includes everything from encouragement to specific skills training.

Many companies have internal training programs. Find out what they are and how to get your people involved. Other companies that do not have internal programs encourage continuing education and training, and often they make arrangements for financial assistance.

Resources

Usually, there is one small holdup in getting your people into a continuing education program that the company will subsidize: budget. In this highly competitive age, there is extreme pressure on budget and the use of resources.

Don't yield to that pressure when it comes to developing your employees. You may save money in the budget for this year, but you will fall behind in gaining highly skilled and able employees for the jobs that you have to do in the future. You will also be robbing your company of better all-around employees.

A positive trend

Although you will probably have to scrape around for the money and justify in triplicate why such training is necessary, go the distance. By doing so, you will accomplish several goals.

First, your employees and the company will see you as a manager who believes in the people working for you. You will motivate your employees. Second, you will set a precedent in your budget for the years to come. The first year of budgeting is often the most difficult. By getting some money now, you will probably be able to get more money in the future. Finally, within a year or two, you will set a standard that other areas of the company will have to live up to. If you begin to have the best trained, most productive employees in the firm, others will have to try to catch up with you. And you'll be positioned as a strong leader and a trendsetter.

Best of all, as these things all begin to form and take shape, your employees will see that you really do believe in them and their abilities. Having faith in them is a very strong motivator. Your employees will go the extra mile to show you that they are worth the extra investment that you are putting into them.

A privilege

As positive as this investment is, it is important to note here that training and education are a privilege and not a right. You should set standards for your employees pertaining to these opportunities. If they are going to a university for work toward a degree, you should have a minimum grade level set for reimbursement. You want to instill in your employees that you expect them to work as diligently at their education as they do at their jobs.

For professional seminars and workshops, you should

meet with employees when they return and discuss new skills or concepts that they learned. Ask them to develop a plan for you as to how they will apply what they learned. Some seminars may prove to be less valuable than others. If that was the case, you need to come to some understanding with the employees about finding something valuable from the training to apply to their situation. Don't make the mistake of sending other employees to the same training program.

CHAPTER 43

Remember special days

*R*emembering special occasions lets employees know that they are appreciated. It seems like such a small thing that many managers overlook this opportunity to give extra encouragement. But as in most things of life, attention to the small things makes the big things happen.

Personal touch

The president of one company sends a letter to an employee on the birthday and on the anniversary of employment. He has a standard form for each letter, but he always includes something personal in it. From time to time, he handwrites an additional note at the bottom of the letter. Employees know it's an automated process, but they appreciate the fact that he cares enough to set up the system and think about them.

Develop a list of people who work for you. Contact the human resources department for some vital information such as birthdays and hire dates. If you don't have a human resources department, either you or your assistant can go to the people directly and get the information. Fill in on your calendar all the days you want to remember with these people.

Go to a card store, and buy a supply of cards that you can give at the appropriate times. If you have a supply of cards, you won't be caught unaware.

Check your calendar each week. Take a few minutes and fill out a card for everyone with a special day that week. You don't have to be overly sentimental, but be personal in the note. If a special day falls on a weekend, give the card to the employee on the Friday before the event.

Party time

You may want to consider having a small party once a month for everyone with a birthday that month. That way, you can reduce the number of parties throughout the month, giving you a better opportunity to manage the time taken up in celebrations. And you will also avoid the chance of appearing to play favorites by giving someone a special party but forgetting to recognize someone else.

Low-tech approach in a high-tech world

Recognizing that the people who work for you have special days in their lives will communicate to them that you care about them as individuals, not just as cogs in the machine to get work done. It's one way to offset the high-tech trend that allows for less and less contact with others.

In this environment you must exert the extra effort to apply what John Naisbitt in his book *Megatrends* calls *high touch*. The more you can show employees that you care about all the aspects of their lives, the more loyalty and contentment you can develop. If you think this is a waste of time, try it for a year. You will see that remembering people on special occasions will raise morale or at the very least help you maintain it at a high level.

CHAPTER 44

Involve employees in special groups

*O*ne of the goals that you want to accomplish with your employees is to get them to see the impact of their jobs on the organization as a whole. You want them to think in a wider sphere than the responsibilities that they currently hold. There are a number of ways to foster this, but an effective way is to involve employees in groups in which you participate within your company.

Meetings

As a manager, you take part in meetings that involve your peers as well as your superiors. In the meetings you discuss many issues, including such things as the progress of other areas of the company and problems facing the company or your area specifically. If you can work it out, bring guests to the meetings so that they can hear about issues facing the organization that they may not have thought about before.

If you work in sales, get some of your employees exposed to what the people in research and development are dealing with. If you work in manufacturing, get your employees involved so that they can hear about the financial pressures affecting the company.

By allowing people in your area to be exposed to problems challenging the company at a higher level, you accomplish a couple of things. First, you expose employees to issues that are beyond the normal bounds of responsibility. That can help as they look at their jobs and see how they fit into the bigger picture. Second, the self-esteem of employees will rise because they feel that you believe in them enough to show them what's happening in other areas of the company.

Projects

Perhaps there are large projects that you get involved in. Maybe you must negotiate a new contract with a vendor. Involving employees in this process with you will allow them to see some of the pressures you face and prepare them for the day when they must step in to carry some of that responsibility.

Passive contributions

Employees should not go to a meeting or learn about a project believing that it is theirs or that they should become actively involved. Obviously, they can discuss the group's activities with you at a later time and offer suggestions for you to present.

Permit as many employees as possible to join in this kind of activity. To select one person and consistently give the employee the opportunity will breed a contempt of that employee by fellow workers. However, you do not have to include everyone in an equal number of activities. Some employees who are moving up in the organization will need more experience.

CHAPTER 45

Empower employees

As a general rule, to motivate employees to take more responsibility for their work, empower them. Give them the power to do their jobs as they see fit within the boundaries you set for them. Once you have trained your employees about a job and how it fits into the bigger picture, and you have helped them understand the values that you hold for getting a job done, give them the authority and the responsibility to get it done as best they can.

More than one way

Many bosses want things done only the way that they would do them. Of course, that is always the prerogative of a boss. But if you can give employees the chance to do things their way, within the parameters that you have set, they will have more ownership of the job that they are responsible for. And empowerment will give your employees ownership.

A boost to enthusiasm

If you need to have something done a certain way, explain it to those whose job it is to perform the task. But if there is flexibility in how something gets done, step out of the loop, and let the creativity and enthusiasm of employees take hold. You may feel uncomfortable at first, but in the end the people in your workforce will believe they are in charge of getting the job done, and they will assume the responsibility to get it done in the best way possible.

Reduced workload

The great payoff for you as the boss in this environment is twofold. First, employees will be motivated to improve the way things are done. Second, employees will take some of the workload off your shoulders. They will begin to make decisions on their own instead of coming to you for every decision. You will be free to spend more time developing your employees and planning. The work flow will become more streamlined, and things will get done faster and oftentimes better than if you have to control everything in your area of responsibility.

When things get done more quickly and more efficiently, you have time to plan new activities that will enhance the productivity of your area.

So, when you are faced with getting a job done, give your employees the chance to do it their way within the boundaries that you set for them. They will make mistakes, but that is OK. Mistakes can be fixed, and people learn a lot more when they have the chance to make mistakes that are theirs, not their boss's. Empowered people are motivated and productive people.

CHAPTER 46

Evaluate potential

*W*e have already discussed the significance of evaluating the abilities of your employees. It is very important to evaluate the job that your employees are doing in light of what they are capable of. Setting an arbitrary standard for employees is easy, but that doesn't really serve anyone. Obviously, you need to have a minimum standard for each job, but what about employees who can perform at a far higher level than the minimum?

And equally demotivating to employees are unrealistically high standards. In doing the job, they will feel that they will never be able to make the grade. Then they will quit trying.

Walk a tightrope

You have to set a minimum standard, and you also have to evaluate what you expect from each employee as it relates to the job. Sometimes you will have to be painfully honest with employees about their potential in a certain job. Of course, in talking with them, you should always let them know of your willingness to try to move them to a position that does play to their strengths.

Another thing to evaluate—and it is often not taken into

consideration—is how employees feel about their potential or their expectations for a specific job. Some people are driven to succeed. Others want to move up the ladder simply for the money that a higher level will offer. But some employees like what they are doing, don't want more stress, and are happy staying put in the current job.

Maintain status quo?

These stay-put employees can present a challenge. As a manager, you can be comfortable leaving them where they are, but you can, over time, experience guilt about their staying at the same level. You have two options to consider. The first is to accept their desire to stay at a certain level, whatever the reason. The second is to work with them over a period of time, stretch them, and see if you can instill a desire in them to grow to new levels of responsibility and productivity.

As a boss, you cannot tell all employees that they can move up the ladder, quickly or not. That would violate the principle of honesty. Some people will be more inclined to move up, and others will not put forth the effort or show the growth needed to move up. You must be realistic and honest with each employee about the future.

Watch for change

This evaluation of a job and an employee's abilities should constantly evolve. Things change. Perhaps something will change for an employee, and he will begin to grow. Maybe she will overcome a hurdle in her personal life that will allow her to dream big dreams about her career. And the jobs that you need to have done will change, too. So whatever evaluation you make, recognize that it, too, will evolve. The need for ongoing dialogue is crucial.

Don't try to rush this process. It will take careful evaluation, clear thinking, and a truly caring boss to initiate a plan to evaluate employees' potential for the future.

CHAPTER 47

Be open to innovative ideas

*H*ow do bosses react when employees present lots of new ideas about how things can be done or new things to try? Some bosses are threatened, others are afraid of change, and still others don't want to change the function of a job that they once held.

If you are truly going to develop employees, they must feel that they have some power over the way things get done. A boss who stonewalls good, innovative ideas reinforces employees' restraint of productive ideas and their powerlessness over work life. Employees are discouraged from becoming invested in the jobs that they have to accomplish.

One boss said that he encouraged employees to come forth with new or innovative ideas. But it seemed that each time an employee began to share an idea, he asked negative questions or had any number of reasons that the idea wouldn't work. It wasn't long before employees stopped sharing ideas. Things didn't change much because everyone figured the boss knew how he wanted things done, and despite his talk, he didn't really want to hear what employees had to say.

Not an automatic yes

There are good reasons *not* to try specific ideas. They may go beyond the budget you have available. They may interfere with other areas of the company, and you will have to win the approval of those areas before initiating a change. Thus, being open to innovative ideas is not saying yes to every idea that comes along.

What is important is the trend in your thinking. Do you automatically dismiss some ideas because of the employees who had them? Or because of the cost? Are you uncomfortable changing the way things have always been done? If so, you likely squelch most good ideas that come your way. Eventually, the ideas will quit coming your way.

Never "good enough"

When ideas quit coming your way because there is a lack of motivation by employees, you are on the verge of being in deep trouble. Having no new ideas means that everything is "good enough," and we have already discussed how deadly these words can be to the morale and growth of your employees.

Carefully evaluate each idea on its own merit, regardless of what it involves and whom it came from. If you feel uncomfortable with an idea, ask yourself why. Does it make business sense? Does it violate a principle you have established? Do you not want to change the status quo? Are you afraid to incur the wrath of your boss if it doesn't work?

The discomfort factor

Knowing where your discomfort comes from will give you a good start on dealing with it. If everything makes sense to you but you still don't want to move ahead because of your discomfort, remember the leadership value of doing the right thing, no matter what the cost. We tend to assume the cost will not involve our personal discomfort, but it may.

So encourage employees to bring you innovative ideas, consider them, and then decide which ones you can use. You may have to wait on some, but share that with your employees. It may be a year before you can initiate certain changes, but get them in your plan. Be open to changes from your employees.

CHAPTER 48

Develop career paths

A career path is a hot topic these days. So what is it? A career path is an explanation of how an employee can develop within an organization. Each position should equip an employee to develop skills that will open up other job opportunities. Most organizations, except some very small companies, have entry-level positions. When that job is mastered, an employee should know what other jobs will be available.

Options

A career path is much like a track of courses in school. You start at a certain place, and by the choices you make, you move from a general course of studies to a more specific course. Early on in a track of courses you have some options of where you would like to go. The farther into a track you go, the more narrow and in-depth the courses become. It's the same with a job. A person at an entry-level position has a number of options available. A vice president of finance is fairly limited in the options available.

Some bosses are reluctant to discuss available options because they don't know how quickly they will be able to implement a promotion or job change. They are afraid of making promises that they can't keep—and rightfully so. But to discuss options is not to make promises. Nearly all employees will want to know what kind of future they have with a company if they work hard, grow, develop their skills, and hang in there.

Creating a reasonable career path for an employee will take some time and consideration of the present positions available within an area. In fact, it should include every position that you are responsible for. If an employee takes a specific position, what will then be the options after the person masters that job?

To help a person develop and reach maximum potential, you need to help the employee set goals, learn, develop, and work hard to get to the next level. To allow employees to sit in blind unawareness of what they can look forward to will demotivate them. They won't believe that you are looking out for them, they will begin to feel trapped, and they will lose their motivation to excel.

Small vs. large

If you work in a small company, you want to let employees know what they can look forward to, but things are small enough that everyone is aware of the potential in a job. You can talk about the next stages of the company. If the company grows, will those who work for you have opportunities to grow in responsibility? In a large company, people can grow up the corporate ladder; in a small company, people grow not necessarily in position, but in authority and responsibility.

Be sure that when you discuss career paths you talk in terms of what could be, what skills employees will need to learn, and what direction they are going, not in terms of promises for future positions.

CHAPTER 49

Develop the whole employee

*T*oo many managers focus only on the skills that will make employees more productive on the job. They don't take into account that many employees are interested in growing as individuals as well. The managers fail to take into consideration the higher level of satisfaction and productivity that employees may have if they are growing in all areas of their lives, not just in their careers.

Personal skills

Of course, it is not an employer's duty to take on the responsibility for an employee's nonwork life. It is really not the domain of an employer. However, it is the concern of an employer if helping an employee develop personal skills can make the employee more effective on the job.

Perhaps you have a promising employee who never got a college diploma. Maybe you have employed someone who needs help with money management. Perhaps an employee has emotional problems or substance abuse problems. All of these personal issues can have a dramatic effect on the development of the employee. Obviously you cannot be responsible for every individual's personal problems. But if they are affecting his work, you must deal with it.

Wise financial moves

Many larger companies are taking notice of these issues. They sponsor higher education reimbursement programs. They bring in experts to conduct seminars on personal money management, or they provide special counseling programs to help employees through personal crises. They even have special programs for employees who are struggling with substance abuse.

These companies are not throwing their money away. The more they can help their employees become more complete, well-rounded individuals, the more productive they believe these employees will be in the workplace.

Balance in life

In our competitive marketplace, it is critical to realize that the employers attracting the best employees take into consideration the lifestyle and development of employees and help them find the appropriate balance between work and personal life.

As a boss, you may not have the resources of your company available. Part of your job will be to lobby the company about which programs would be most useful. Even if your company never does implement these value-added services, you can look around your community and find out what programs are available for your employees if they need additional training in areas that are more personal than professional. No company can afford every program. Be resourceful in finding organizations for substance abuse, literacy programs, credit counseling services, and so on.

By working with your employees in areas that help their personal lives, you will be helping yourself as a manager and your company.

CHAPTER 50

Be an example
with your own boss

One way to teach your employees about how to act with you as a boss is to show them that there are ways to approach certain issues, to grow and develop. It is called *modeling* in the world of psychology. Modeling is a term used for doing things in a specific way, hoping to influence others to deal with issues in the same way.

Probing questions

For example, a man left one company to go to another. After a short time, he realized that the management style of his new boss was less than he had hoped for. Instead of leaving that job, he decided to help his new boss get better, but he knew he couldn't tell the new boss what had to change.

The new boss paid little attention to detail, and he expected everyone to know what he was thinking. So the man began to ask questions of clarification of his boss to make his own job easier. When an assignment was made, he would ask about when the work had to be completed, what form the work should take, and so on. Soon, the boss knew the questions would be coming, and he became more specific in his assignments. The man had begun to effectively manage his relationship with his boss.

Positive interaction

The absolute best way to influence your employees is to model for them how employees should act. You have a boss, and the way you interact with your boss will be a strong factor in how your employees believe they should interact with you. This is true whether or not you like your boss, your boss works to develop you, or you get along with your boss.

If you can show enthusiasm, not complain about the decisions that your boss makes regarding your work, and treat your boss with the respect that the position deserves, those who work for you will see that you are living out the very things that you are encouraging them to live out.

Famous models

This entire concept is seen throughout our society when we talk about movie stars, politicians, and athletes as role models for kids. If kids can have a hero who deals with life in an exceptional way, we hope that the role model will exert some sort of influence on them. The same is true in a much more intense manner concerning the people you work with. Although you may not be in the national spotlight, you have one major advantage over public figures. You have daily contact. Your example is not that of some distant person others want to emulate. You are not a person they hear about every few weeks or months. Your example is regular and repeated.

You will be a role model whether you want to be one or not. Your attitudes, beliefs, and actions will be watched, learned from, and emulated whether you want them to be or not. So if you are going to teach others how to act in the workplace, you must recognize that you are a teacher by experience.

Rather than fight it, use it to your advantage. Develop yourself. Act out the values that you say you believe. Show enthusiasm for your work. Treat people with respect, and they will treat you with respect.

CHAPTER 51

Write a statement of purpose

Your company probably has a statement of purpose. If it doesn't, be a proponent of getting one written as soon as possible. It is just as important for you as a boss to have a statement of purpose for what you do.

You have a list of values that are vital for you to communicate to employees. You have a job description that lays out the responsibilities of your job. You know what you think is important in being a great boss. And in this book, you have learned several ways to help you be a great boss.

Refine it

Take all of this information and write it out. It may be a very long piece. Start right away to take all the information and boil it down into general statements about what you need and want to accomplish in doing your job.

It may take a while, and you probably can't do it in one sitting. It will take reflection to synthesize all of the specifics into some general guidelines. But if you eventually condense your statement of purpose to two or three paragraphs that encompass all the specifics that you are responsible for, you will have a guide that will help you make decisions about what is significant and whether or not an activity falls into the purpose you are trying to fulfill.

Memorize it

A statement of purpose is the kind of document that you will ultimately memorize because you will refer to it so often. It should help you establish the things that are most fundamental in being a great boss.

A statement of purpose is really your chance to articulate your philosophy of management as it applies to your current job. Since it is philosophical, though, you will find that if you advance or change jobs, much of what you come up with will transfer because the statement of purpose bears more on who you are than on what you do.

Implement it

A good statement of purpose needs to be short and general. It should talk about your objectives as a manager, not your specific duties. A statement of purpose would read something like this: "My job as a manager is to provide a stable, pleasant working environment where every worker is valued and appreciated. It is also to provide an environment where employees are challenged to continually better themselves, encouraged to become the best they can be, and presented with excellence as their standard."

A statement of purpose should not be a list of specifics like this: "My responsibility as a manager is to control budgets, run meetings, hire personnel, and make sure that each employee is contributing to the company's well-being by performing each and every item on the job description."

Having a statement of purpose in place will guide you to appropriate goals for yourself and for your employees.

CHAPTER 52

Set annual development goals

We have talked about the importance of goals and the need to stretch people. We have talked about quantifying jobs so that employees know that you want them to strive for excellence. Just as basic is having programs with employees so that they know you are serious about their development.

Personalized plan

Look at each job in relation to the employee doing that job. Are there skills that he needs to acquire? If so, find ways to encourage him to get the training that will make him better. Don't wait for him to come to you and ask to go to a workshop or seminar. Write it into a yearly plan. Make it a part of the performance evaluation. Let the employee know that you expect him to find ways to get the training he needs.

A saying declares, "You don't get what you want; you get what you measure." If that is indeed true, you will find employees much more willing to expand their knowledge and skills if they know they will be evaluated on these items at the end of each year.

In one company a group of employees brought up the idea

of development goals. With some effort they finally convinced their boss to allow them to have an annual plan for training and personal development. It became a part of their standards of performance, and they were not considered to have completed their jobs unless they met their development goals as well as their specific job functions. They began to feel valued and motivated.

Reports

When you expect people to find ways to get training and when you need to have some way of evaluating the effectiveness of their training, you should probably have some sort of report that they fill out after a training experience. This reporting system will help you emphasize that training opportunities are not chances to get away from work but they are parts of work.

Sit down and go over it with them on their return. Find out what they learned. Ask them if they would recommend this training to others in your area. If they learned something especially good or applicable, ask them to share with others on your team what they learned.

It is your responsibility to be sure that each employee has a developmental plan. Analyze the areas that each person needs to focus on. And when you come up with a plan, write it down so that the employee knows and agrees on the goals for the next year.

Opportunities

It is not your responsibility to discover every opportunity for every employee. Certainly, you should keep your eyes open and pass on opportunities to the right employee. Make sure that the budget and time are available for the employee to fulfill the plan you come up with. But the execution of the plan, just like the job, is the responsibility of the employee. Development is not an extra; the plan makes it a part of the job.

If you don't plan for things, they won't happen. Other urgent items will always fill the time. If you don't plan for the development of your people, it won't happen. They will be the poorer for your not doing your part in planning, and you will be the poorer for not having the best-trained employees you could have.

Devlin Donaldson works with Compassion International and has written for *Marriage Partnership* magazine.